fun loving girl's

guide to parties

First published in Great Britain by HarperCollins Publishers Ltd in 2003

1 3 5 7 9 10 8 6 4 2

0-00-715222-1

Bang on the door character copyright:
© 2003 Bang on the Door all rights reserved.
bang on the door ™© is a trademark
Exclusive right to license by Santoro
www.bangonthedoor.com
Text © 2003 HarperCollins Publishers Ltd.

Printed and bound in Hong Kong

fun loving girl's

guide to parties

I just **love** to party, don't you? Not sure which kind of party to have? Never fear, **fun loving girl** is here! Read some of my fab and funky party ideas and make sure your 'do' is the one that no one forgets! Also, find out how to make the coolest party invites and guarantee your name's always on the guest list for the next... and the next.

let's party!

party invitation

from: fun loving girl

to: groovy guy

place: my place

date & time: saturday! 8.00pm

1. Tip one... The party list!
2. What kind of party?
3. Make a date!
4. Who to invite
5. Decide the decor
6. Organise nibbles
7. Games
8. Shop for outfit!

POP!

perfect guest or

Are you the girl guaranteed to make any party swing or the one who watches the fun from the sofa? Try our fun quiz and see how you rate in the party invite stakes.

1 The invite says 'come as your favourite character'. Do you:

a) go as yourself?
b) go as your favourite pop diva?
c) wear a fake fur coat and go as a teddy?

2 No one's dancing. Do you:

a) take over the dance floor with your cool moves?
b) grab some friends and get them all dancing with you?
c) wait for others to start and join in later?

3 Your pal hands out green jelly. You hate jelly, so you...

a) ...say "yuk!"
b) ...say "Oooh, it's too pretty to eat!"
c) ...leave it on a chair or table!

party pooper?

4 At a sleepover, you're tired but your friends are still partying. Do you:

a) put on some groovy music?
b) splash your face with water?
c) brush your teeth and slip in to bed?

5 There's a quiet moment at a friend's party. Do you:

a) throw some popcorn and start a food fight?
b) play a game and get everyone giggling?
c) put on a video and chill out?

6 It's your turn to sing at a karaoke party. Do you:

a) go for it – you love to perform?
b) get some of your pals to do a girl band tune with you?
c) get out of it by saying you can't sing?

perfect guest or party pooper?

Add up your score and check out
how you did below!

Mostly a

You are certainly a riot at a party. You'd do anything for a laugh but sometimes your games and jokes can be a bit too crazy! Be careful you don't go too far!

Mostly b

You're the sort of guest who's always ready to join in, and you like to make sure that your friends have a great time too! Watch out for more invites in the post!

Mostly c

Do you really like parties? Sure you do, but you don't need to be the centre of attention. If you feel nervous, look friendly and try and chat to one or two different people and you'll have a great time!

3

get organised!

A party! Great idea, but where do you start? Just watch while I organise my own spectacular bash and learn from the best! You'll soon have your own party under control.

A list will help you make sure you don't forget anything. Tick things off once they're done.

1. Tip one... The party list!
2. What kind of party?
3. Make a date!
4. Who to invite
5. Decide the decor
6. Organise nibbles
7. Games
8. Shop for outfit!

What kind of party?
Well, I love discos! But you don't have to decide now. Wait until you've read my groovy party ideas first!

NIBBLES

Ask Mum to help, and remember plenty of cool drinks too.

MAKE A DATE
Get your parents in on the act. Make sure the date is ok with them first.

august

☀

1 2 3 4 5 6 7 8 9 10 11
12 13 14 15 16 17 18 19 (20)
21 22 23 24 25 26 27
28 20 30 31

party!

guests

THE GUEST LIST
The hardest bit! Deciding the guest list is tricky when you've got sooo many friends you want to see.

5

nised!

MUSIC!

The most important part of a party! Borrow lots of CDs or make a compilation of all your fave songs.

WHAT TO WEAR?

Something sparkly? Dressed up or cool and casual? Better plan a shopping trip now....

Inviting invites

Make your invites look exciting and your party will be too!

I'm making round, silver invites in the shape of CDs. All I need is some silver card and a black pen.

CD

DECORATIONS

Every party needs decorations. No disco lights? No problem! Ask Dad to dig out the fairy lights and hang them around the room. Check out my ideas for more party decorations later on — pages 13-14.

star party

How can you have a truly starry party? Get your friends to come as their favourite pop star! Check out each others' outfits and try to guess who's who!

FILM FUN

Try a film theme where you all dress up as characters from your favourite movie, or just go for a glam movie image – like a secret agents and spies party. Give yourselves spy names like Ivana C. Cret, Donnatella or Heidi Seek.

If you're having a spy party, why not send the invites out in code? Make sure you give plenty of clues!

party...

CLOWNING AROUND

Circus parties are perfect if your friends are always clowning around! Transform the living room into a circus ring and you can be the ringmaster. Get some juggling balls and batons, a plastic plate and a long stick for plate spinning, and hoop to spin around your waist.

FAIR'S FAIR

Set up sideshows and invite your friends to roll up, roll up. Try a coconut shy – propping a coconut in a small bucket. Pile up some soft balls or bean bags to throw. You'll need some little prizes for the winners.

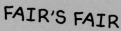

8

COOL DUDE DO

How about a beach barbecue in your own garden? Fill a paddling pool and bring out the sandpit and deckchairs! Ask Dad to rustle up hotdogs and burgers on the barbie and dress as surf dudes and dudettes...

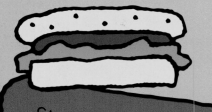

stylish sleepovers

Choose three best pals and get busy with mini-manicures and makeovers.

Sleepover rule 1: stash treats for a midnight feast!

Sleepover rule 2: learn to whisper for late night chats!

Best thing about sleepovers: the party continues the next morning!

Worst thing about sleepovers: you have to tidy your room afterwards!

party...

THINK PINK

If it's a pretty in pink party, line up the strawberry milkshakes and pink iced cake!

timezone

70s parties mean hilarious outfits! Look for orange flared trousers and brown tank tops.

Lovely! Try charity shops.

Make a splash with a swimming party! Most public pools are available for hire for 20 or so friends. Though if you're inviting about eight, you don't need to hire or book in advance – just take along a couple of grown-ups. Go for pools with water slides and wave machines for maximum fun!

Why stop there? If the coast isn't too far away, plan a trip to the beach! Organise a party picnic and grab a beach ball for games on the sand.

Hiring a party venue is a great idea if you live in a small apartment or you want to be able to invite lots of pals. Ice skating or roller skating rinks are perfect – and they often let you take along your favourite music!

11

a difference

Have a trampoline party and your friends will all be jumping for joy! An instructor usually comes with the trampoline hire at local sports halls, so she/he'll teach you all the tricks.

Aim high and hire a basket-ball court. There's nothing like it for team spirit. Again, an instructor will usually organise the game and give you tips.

Live life in the fast lane and head for the nearest bowling alley. Hire one or two lanes next to each other (six play on one lane, usually) and see who scores a strike.

Don't forget!

Bring plenty of drinks — partying is thirsty work.

12

parties with

Once you've got your reason to party, make your room look the part. Colour theme parties are easy.

Just hang up balloons, strings of ribbons and streamers. Use coloured table-cloths.

get the look!

13

model mayhem

Fashion parties are
SO trendy!
Set up a rail or area for
clothes and a rug for the
catwalk. Hang a string of
fairy lights around a mirror
and gather cosmetics and
hair stuff for the make-up
corner. Ask your friends to
bring fun outfits, make-up,
hair accessories and their
own brushes and get
together for a fashion show
you'll never forget!

Don't forget!

Think about the
lighting. Fairy lights
are fab, the more
the merrier, string
them across walls
and around chairs.
A few lamps placed
in corners work
just as well.

yumm*y*

tasty treats are essential! Clever cookies serve up food that gets guests talking!

Try these...

FRUIT SMILES

Simple but smiley! Cut slices of oranges and melon into wide smiles (semi-circle shapes) and arrange on a plate. They make for great photos and are good for breaking the ice.

PIZZAS WITH PIZZAZZ!

Buy some ready-made mini pizza bases. Spread them with tomato paste and cover with mozzarella or grated cheese. Pop on two olives for eyes, and a thin, curved slice of red pepper for a smile! Bake in a hot oven for 9–11 minutes.

15

party snacks

PARTY CAKE
You can buy a cake and add some coloured icing!

BERRY NICE INDEED

You'll need a grown-up to help you. First break a large bar of chocolate into pieces and place in a bowl, stand the bowl inside a pan of hot water, and stir regularly until the chocolate melts. Wash the strawberries and carefully dip them in the melted chocolate then stand them on greaseproof paper. Yummy!

For added sparkle, add sparklers to your food! Remember to check that the sparklers are ok for indoor use. Push the sparklers into cakes, ice cream or a tub of sand in the centre of your table, let the grown-ups light them, stand back and say oohh!

FUNKY FRUITY KEBABS

Stick chunks of fruit on sticks and you've got fruit kebabs! Easy!

Don't forget! Have a bucket of water handy to drop used sparklers in, as the ends get very hot.

A cocktail party is so sophisticated. But you have to plan and buy the ingredients for your concoctions and don't forget the decorations! Dress code — seriously posh!

LEMON FIZZ

Fill wide brimmed cocktail glasses with fizzy lemonade and add a squeeze of lemon juice. Thread one or two strawberries onto a cocktail stick and rest it in the glass. Wet the rim of the glass and carefully sprinkle caster sugar so that it sticks around the rim. Pop in a straw. For a red fizz, mix in some cranberry juice.

SUNSHINE PUNCH

Mix half a glass of orange juice with half pineapple juice and swirl with a swizzle stick. Add a straw, and balance a cocktail stick with a cherry and a chunk of pineapple on it across the top of the glass. Pop in a cocktail umbrella to finish it off!

ails

BANANA SMOOTHIE

So yummy they'll be back for more and more! Whizz (in a blender) a banana with two thirds of a glass of milk and a scoop of vanilla ice cream. Serve with ice-cubes and a straw.

Don't forget!

★ wooden cocktail sticks

★ crushed ice

★ selection of fruit cut into bite sized pieces

★ umbrellas or swizzle sticks

18

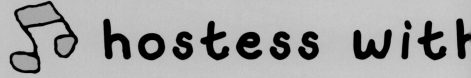

♫♪ hostess with

Try some of my tricks to make sure it's
the event of the year!

Form your own band! Choose your band members
and get together to rehearse beforehand. Play
instruments, if you can, or lip-sync your way
to stardom by miming to your favourite tune.

Host a pop stars contest. Just
play some chart songs and
sing along karaoke-style.
You could even hire a karaoke machine
but a CD player will do fine. If you have
some pals that play instruments, even better!

Don't forget!

Give a little party gift so friends have something to
take away or take a snap shot of them at the party,
perhaps singing on stage, skating or posing on a catwalk if
it's a fashion party. Email or send it to them later.

19

he mostess!

Try a comedy club. Create a stage and take turns telling jokes. If you aren't sure your pals know enough jokes, have a joke book handy!

How about a lucky dip? Just wrap up some little pressies, like chocolate bars, woven bracelets, hair slides and cute-shaped mini soaps. Hide them in a basket or tub of your hamster's straw.

PARTY DOs AND DON'Ts

☆ Do chat to as many people as possible!

☆ Do borrow lots of CDs or tape your fave party tunes.

☆ Do ask guests if they need a drink or snack.

☆ Don't keep playing the same songs!

☆ Don't spend the evening texting!

☆ Don't leave anyone out of the fun and games!

☆ Don't stay up too late. Even the best parties come to an end!

party

Fun Loving Girl says, "Parties are all about having lots of fun things to do. Try some groovy games — you won't stop giggling!".

PASS THE BALLOON (NOT USING HANDS)!
You need a balloon and everyone to stand in a circle. Start with the balloon under someone's arm. They try to pass it to the next party girl, who passes it to the next in the circle and so on.

POP PICKERS' PARTY...
Divide everyone into teams and play just the beginning of songs. Which team can guess the record from the first few notes?

GUESS THE GUEST
Blindfold someone and the rest of you all run around. Now the blindfolded person has to try and find a guest and guess who it is!

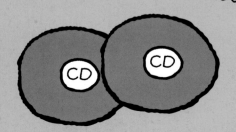

CD CD

games

CATCH THE CATCHPHRASE?
Write down some lines from hit records. Read them out and see which team can guess the song they come from?
Film fans may prefer to choose lines from famous movies, or catchphrases from cartoons.

BOARD GAMES ARE FUN!

Why not make a huge, floor version of snakes and ladders

Just tape sheets of paper together and draw eight squares (big enough to stand on) across and eight down. Number them and draw snakes and ladders between them. Roll a dice and play like normal.

CHARADES
A good old fave! Is it a film, TV programme, book or video game? Show each other the number of words in the title — then act it out!

Fun Loving Girl says –
don't let dressing up get you down! Next time you feel a party
outfit panic coming on – breathe deeply and follow my tips...

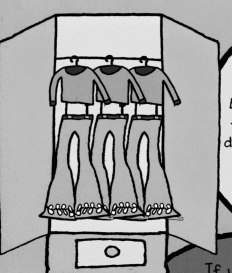

First find out if there is a dress code... You don't want to be the only partygoer in a frock at a skateboarders' do, or turn up in jeans when everyone's in party dresses! Oops...

Go for sparkly sequin tops or little dresses.

If you've bought new shoes, put them on a few times before the party to wear them in – you'll never get into the groove with blisters on your toes!

Don't forget! Pick your outfit carefully – make sure it's something you're comfortable in – you have to wear it all night!

23

ll I wear?

Changing your hairstyle to really get noticed! It's amazing what a slick of gel and a funky flower or clip can do, or pull all your hair into a topknot, leaving some strands of hair hanging loose at the front.

How about a denim skirt and some glam tights? Leopard print tights are purr-fect, and glittery ones look great.

Always have a party outfit ready and waiting in your wardrobe. You never know when you might get a last minute invitation!

Take your time to decide and check with pals — you don't all want to turn up looking exactly the same.

Dress up your favourites with some cool accessories. A large belt slung low around your hips, or party sandals or boots with a skirt instead of trainers.

For a pop diva look, shades are good.

Parties are always a great excuse to get glammed up! Try some sparkly body glitter.

24

get read

Sometimes the best bit about going to a party is the getting ready! Invite over a friend or two and have a pre-party party. You can try on all your clothes and get ready together.

Ask your pals to bring extra accessories and hair bits with them, then you can all share, and don't let them forget their hair and make-up brushes.

o party

As you get ready, have a mini fashion show! You can practise your dance moves at the same time!

or a wavy look, dampen your hair, then plait it in a mixture of small and thicker plaits. Dry it off with a hair dryer and leave it to cool. Later, when you're nearly ready, take out the plaits and gently separate the curls with your fingers. It will be wavy and full.

Parties are a chance to shine. For sparkly shoulders, dab on a little bit of body glitter. Then add some teeny stars to your cheeks.

Smooth eyebrows gently so the hairs lay flat making you look groomed! Try it.

Dab a teeny bit of shimmery gloss to your lips. It keeps them soft, too!

top 10 ways to get the party started

Need to break the ice? Try these conversation starters and things you can do to get you and your guests in the mood for fun.

If it's your party...

Look around to check for people on their own, and dash over to say hello.

Introduce people to each other and say something about them so they get chatting... such as "Judy's got a pet snake, ask her what it eats..."

Don't play the music so loud that everyone's shouting to be heard!

If it's a funky record, organise a team dance and get everyone on their feet.

Organising games is a great way of getting people involved. Check out my games and entertainments ideas (pages 21/22) and have some ready!

Think of a fun way of introducing yourself like, "Hi, I'm Fun Loving Girl, I like eating bagels, doing cartwheels and partying — but not all at the same time!"

What to say to people you don't know... "Hi, I'm sure I've seen you somewhere before — Oh, I remember, you're in my maths class..."

Ask people questions about themselves to get them talking and you'll soon find you have something in common.

27

just joking

If in doubt, tell a joke...
Try some of the ones on this page...

Everyone likes someone who looks happy!

smile!

Why did the teenager cross the road? His parents told him not to!

Did you hear about the skeleton and his girlfriend? They broke up. He was shattered!

How do you know if an elephant's been in your fridge? He's left footprints in the trifle!

Why did the girl take a mushroom to the party? He was a fungi to have around!

Waiter, waiter, do you serve crabs here? We serve anyone, sit down!

Why is Cinderella useless at football? She's got a pumpkin for a coach!

28

  surprise

Make sure everyone can keep a secret!

parT nxt Sat? Can u handle the invts?

Organise yourselves! Either one person has to take control and organise the whole event, or everyone has to take on a different area to organise, such as invites, food, music, venue...

It's best not to plan a themed surprise party, as it's unlikely that the surprise party girl will turn up in the right style!

29

arties

Get her family in on the act, so you know she will be free to come to *her* party! And if it's going to be at her home, you'll definitely need their help!

Try to avoid whispering about the party as *she* draws near — she may think you're up to something!! (Or she may get the wrong idea and get upset!)

"shush everyone!"

Arrange for everyone to get to the party at least 20 minutes before party girl arrives. AND get them all to be quiet so tell-tale giggles don't give the game away!

"surprise...!"

Make sure you've got a good excuse for keeping party girl away from the surprise beforehand..."I've just remembered, I didn't say goodbye to my cat..."

...and an excuse for going to the party without giving away the secret.

30

what kind of party would suit you?

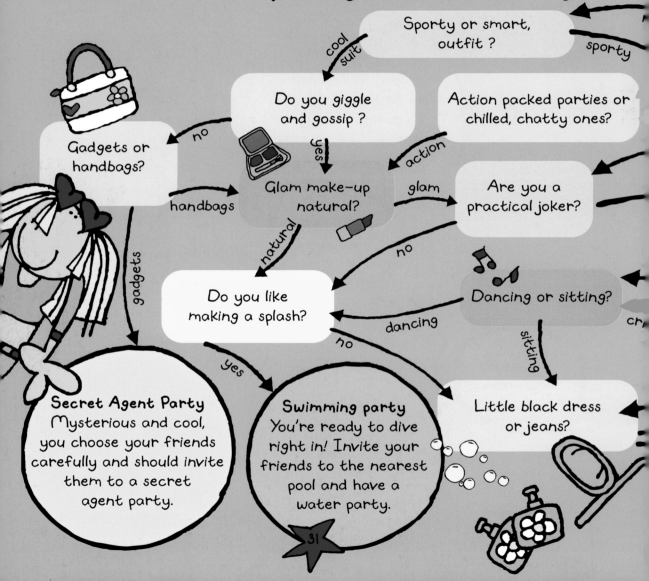

Sporty or smart, outfit?

cool suit

sporty

Do you giggle and gossip?

Action packed parties or chilled, chatty ones?

Gadgets or handbags?

no

yes

action

handbags

Glam make-up natural?

glam

Are you a practical joker?

gadgets

natural

no

Do you like making a splash?

Dancing or sitting?

dancing

cr

sitting

yes

no

Secret Agent Party
Mysterious and cool, you choose your friends carefully and should invite them to a secret agent party.

Swimming party
You're ready to dive right in! Invite your friends to the nearest pool and have a water party.

Little black dress or jeans?

31

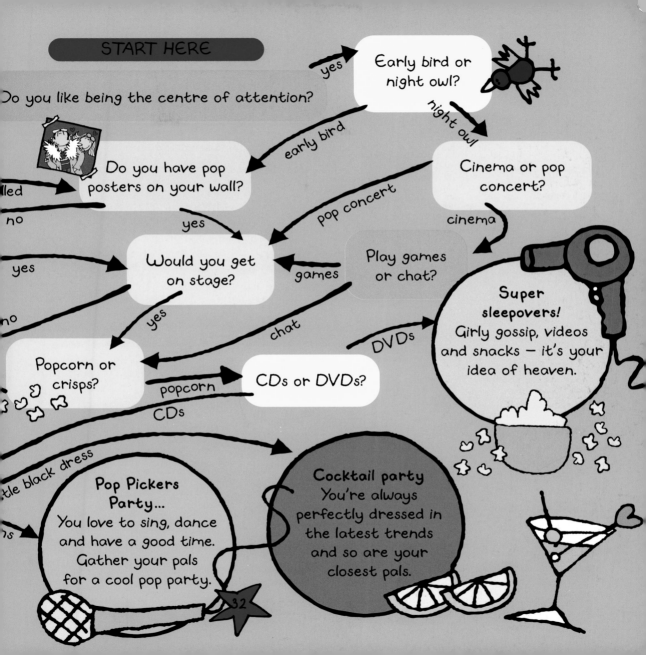

START HERE

Do you like being the centre of attention?

yes → Early bird or night owl?

early bird → Do you have pop posters on your wall?

night owl → Cinema or pop concert?

pop concert

cinema

Do you have pop posters on your wall?

yes → Would you get on stage?

no

lled

Play games or chat?

games → Would you get on stage?

chat

DVDs

yes → Would you get on stage?

yes → Popcorn or crisps?

no

Popcorn or crisps?

popcorn → CDs or DVDs?

CDs

ttle black dress

Super sleepovers!
Girly gossip, videos and snacks — it's your idea of heaven.

Pop Pickers Party...
You love to sing, dance and have a good time. Gather your pals for a cool pop party.

32

Cocktail party
You're always perfectly dressed in the latest trends and so are your closest pals.

groovy

If you're going to a

You could also m

CUTE AS CANDY

Pretty paper boxes filled with sweeties are easy to make. Collect or make little boxes, then decorate them and fill with sweets. Yum!

FURRY FRAMES

You'll need some card, PVA glue and a length of bright fluffy fun fur! Cut out a rectangle of card that measures about 2.5cm larger than the photo – all round. Then cut a smaller rectangle in the centre – about 5mm smaller than the photo. Spread the card frame with PVA glue and stick the fur all round the frame. Carefully stick the photo behind the frame. Gorgeous!

gifts

make a thank you card or pressie with a personal touch.
tle treats to hand guests at your own divine dos!

FAB AND FUNKY JEWELLED MIRROR

What every party going girl needs
— a mirror to look in before she leaves!

You'll need thick card, silver card or foil, scissors, pencil, and PVA glue. Draw and cut out two oval mirror shapes on card — exactly the same size. Cut out the centre of one oval, then cut out an oval piece of silver card or foil that's slightly bigger than the hole. Now stick the silver card/foil, face up in the centre of the plain oval shape, and stick the piece of card with a hole over the top.

Your mirror is now framed.
Paint the frame and decorate. You won't want to give it away!

groovy gifts

FURRY PENCIL CASES

You'll need some biggish bits of furry material, scissors, a ruler, needle and thread and a button.

Ask an adult to help you

Measure and cut a large rectangle from the furry material, (make sure it is longer than your pencil), and fold it in half inside out. Sew up the two shorter edges, being careful not to prick your fingers. Sew the button to the middle of one of the top edges and turn the pencil case the right way round. Opposite the button, which should now be on the inside, cut a slit in the furry material, this will be your buttonhole. The button will make sure nothing falls out of the pencil case.

You now have a fluffy pencil case!

Decorate your pencils by adding strips of fluffy material around the tops with some glue. Now put them in the pencil case.

Your friends will love this gift!

parties around the world!

Some people really know how to throw wild parties! Here are a few brilliant bashes I'd like to have been invited to!

NORTH AMERICAN INDIANS used to party before they went to battle! The tribe members who were about to leave went off and danced together to the sound of drums. This was to muster their courage and to warn enemies nearby that they were ready to battle!

Every year there is a **Violet** Festival in Toulouse, France to celebrate the pretty purple flowers. Awww!

FOOD FIGHT FANS are in for a treat if they head to Northern Spain in August! As part of the very strange **tomatina festival**, vats of squashy tomatoes are set up and everyone throws them at each other!

DRESSING DOWN

In an annual festival in ancient Babylon, the king was stripped of his clothes and sent away! Everyone did as they liked. A few days later he'd return in fine new robes and they'd all behave themselves again!

Every summer, partiers head for the salt flats of Black Rock Desert in Nevada. The Burning Man festival ends by setting light to a fifty foot wooden man, and lots of celebration.

PEOPLE ALL OVER INDIA

go party crazy at Holi, the festival of colour each spring. They get together to celebrate in the streets, dancing and throwing coloured powder (gulal) and water over each other, then everyone heads to the river to get cleaned up.

d the world!

MARDI GRAS

They sure know how to party in New Orleans, USA. Since 1699, carnival season has officially started on January 6 and run through to the parade the Tuesday before Lent – with balls and parties to attend. If you're in the streets for the parades, you're likely to catch "throws" – trinkets, sweets and beads chucked from the floats!

FANTASYFEST is a giant costume party held each autumn in Florida Keys, in America.

38

Why wait for a reason to party?

SEASIDE SPECIAL

It's raining again and you're on holiday! So set up a seaside in your home...Put on the heating, so you can wear your cozzies – you don't even have to apply sun cream! Spread a tablecloth on the floor for your picnic and don't forget to hand round cooling ice-lollies! Warning, people may think you're completely crazy!

BAD HAIR DAY PARTY

Gather friends and hair accessories, plus style ideas from magazines and get to work transforming yourselves. You'll need lots of snacks and drinks, it's hard work!

PLAY IT AGAIN...

If you've got a new CD, invite some friends over to listen to it! You'll soon have a party going on!

CD

39

party time!

PIZZA PARTY

Nothing happening? Then get together with your friends to create pizzas for pleasure. You'll need to organise ingredients for this — and have a parent there to help with the hot oven!

Buy ready-made pizza bases for everyone, and concentrate on the toppings. Slices of red, green and yellow pepper, grated cheese, olives, tomatoes, pepperoni, herbs, and whatever else you may fancy on top of your pizzas.

First spread the base with tomato paste. Then put on some cheese. Now add your chosen toppings. Bake them in the oven for 11–15 minutes, or until the cheese is melted.

Now you can be a groovy chick too!

bang on the door™©

groovy chick's guide to shopping and style

style quiz

fab fashion facts

what to wear

top shopping tips

groovy chick's
guide to shopping and style

Now you can feel fabulous and look groovy at all times! A must for girls with a passion for fashion, this cool guide shows you how to shop smart, mix and match your clothes for those must-have looks and get the style of the stars!

ISBN 0-00-715221-3